HOW CAN I HELP ROLY the HEDGEHOG?

Frances Rodgers & Ben Grisdale

First published in Great Britain in 2020

Editing, design and typesetting by UK Book Publishing

www.ukbookpublishing.com

ISBN: 978-1-8380019-0-2

HOW CAN I HELP ROLY the HEDGEHOG?

Hello, my name is Roly,
I am a hedgehog and I
need your help.

Please let me into your garden. Make me a doorway in your fence.

12cm

I like to eat things I
can find in your garden.

Please plant flowers to
attract the slugs and bugs.

I get very thirsty.

Please leave a small bowl of water out for me.

I can get stuck in rubbish.

Please keep your garden tidy.

BIN

DANGER

Ponds can be a danger to me.

Please give me a ladder
in case I fall in.

BIN

I can also get stuck in nets.

Please lift them up
when not in use.

BIN

I sleep in piles of
leaves and compost.

Please be careful and
look for me first.

BIN

Thank you for all your help.

Now that you know how to help *Roly*, don't forget to help *Rosy*, *Rory* and *Roxy* too!

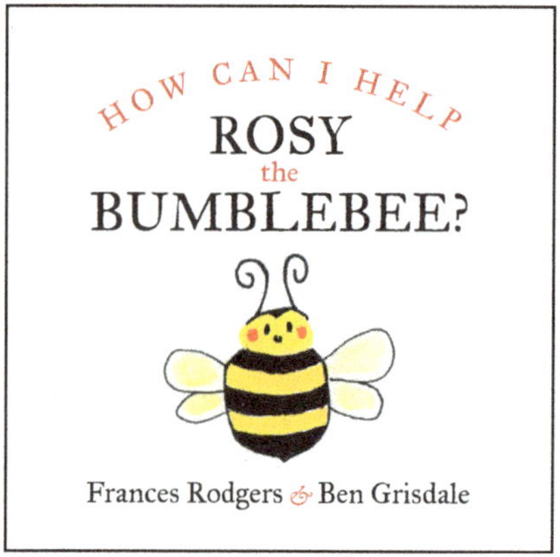

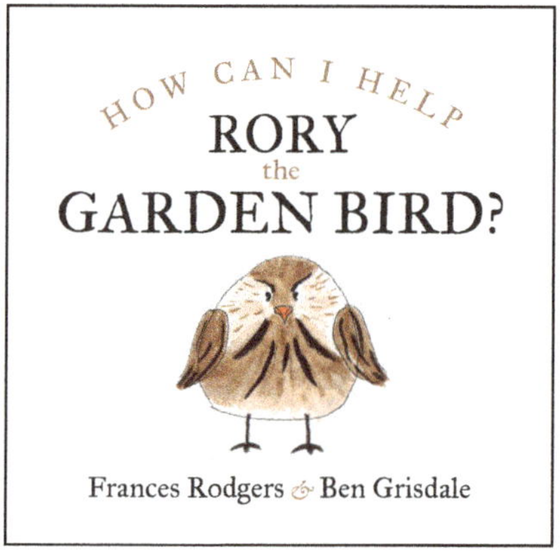

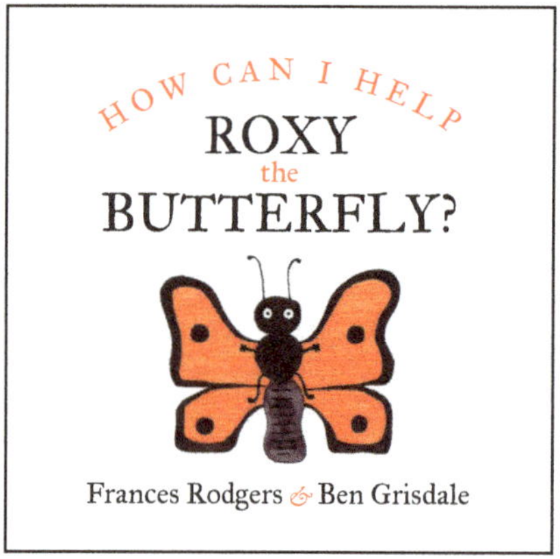

See us on

SAVING BRITAIN'S HEDGEHOGS

CHANNEL 5

Project

Amazing Grace

Build it & we will come

Save Me Trust, Harper Asprey Wildlife Rescue & the British Hedgehog Preservation Society

Now you have seen some of the problems that affect Roly the hedgehog in your garden, please take a look at Project Amazing Grace at *www.gracethehedgehog.co.uk*

Amazing Grace who is Roly's cousin, has many more ways to help hedgehogs in your garden, your school and in the wider community. Watch us on Channel 5 catch-up in 'Meet the hedgehog' and 'Saving Britain's hedgehogs' Episode 1, Episode 2 and Episode 3.

Best wishes

Anne Brummer
Project Amazing Grace
Harper Asprey Wildlife Rescue
Save Me Trust

Lightning Source UK Ltd.
Milton Keynes UK
UKHW051211230920
370340UK00003B/32

9 781838 001902